Dedicated to my Dad and Brother. May you always be buddies. – KB

Acknowledgements:

Kim would like to thank Richard for his invaluable time and expertise in helping to edit the poem. She would also like to thank all the teachers along the way who encouraged her writing. Kim would like to thank her friends and family for their support of her first book "Honey I Love You" which gave her the confidence to publish this second book. She would also like to thank Nic Phelps, Amanda Russell, Greg Triggs, Megan Peretson and Maria Palmiter for being early readers of the book and for their lovely reviews. Finally thank **you** for reading this book and supporting a Canadian author!

Kiddo I Love You

Written by Kim Bunka

Illustrated by Nabeel Hayder

Papa did you love me when I came out of my shell?
Kiddo yes I loved you, with your squawk so like a bell.

Papa do you love me when I waddle on the ice?
Kiddo yes I love you, you don't have to ask me
twice.

Papa do you love me when I splash and swim and dive?
Kiddo yes I love you and I love to see you thrive.

Papa do you love me when I slide down hills of
snow?
Kiddo yes I love you when you slide both fast and
slow

Papa do you love me when you're hunting for our food?

Kiddo yes I love you it's my joy to feed my brood

Papa do you love me when I eat my krill and fish? Kiddo yes I love you, you're the answer to my wish.

Papa do you love me when we take our many walks?

Kiddo yes I love you as we march along and talk.

Papa do you love me when we hug and huddle close?

Kiddo yes I love you when you cuddle on my toes

Papa do you love me when I start to moult and grow?
Kiddo yes I love you when you're going with the flow.

Papa do you love me as I toddle out to sea?
Kiddo yes I love you and you mean so much to
me.

Papa do you love me when I'm swimming far away?
Kiddo yes I love you, in my heart you'll always stay.

Papa do you love me when we watch the Southern Lights?
Kiddo yes I love you throughout all the days and nights.

Emperor Penguins live in Antartica and are the tallest and heaviest of all penguins. They can grow up to 3 feet tall and weigh 50-80 pounds. They have thick layers of shiny waterproof feathers to keep them warm and dry. They can't fly but they are amazing swimmers and dive into the ocean to eat fish, squid and krill. In March the penguins waddle inland to get to the nesting area. The female lays an egg in mid May and then carefully passes the egg to her male partner who keeps the egg warm while the female goes back to the ocean to eat. The chicks hatch in August and the male penguin continues to keep them safe and warm while they wait for the female to come back with food. While they wait they huddle with the other male penguins in colonies of up to five hundred thousand penguins!

Glossary

Antarctica: The continent surrounding the South Pole almost entirely covered by ice.

Brood: Offspring or young, a word used often for baby birds

Colonies: A word used to describe a large group of penguins.

Krill: The small, shrimp-like creatures eaten by animals such as penguins and whales.

Moult: A word meaning to shed feathers, hair, or skin for birds, mammals, and reptiles.

Southern Lights: Beautiful colours that light up the sky in the Southern Hemisphere {for example in Antarctica}.

Thrive: To grow, develop, and be healthy.

Toddle: To move with short unsteady steps.

Waddle: To walk with short steps, swaying or rocking from side to side.

Kim Bunka – Author: Kim lives in beautiful British Columbia, Canada where she is a musical theatre performer and educator. She also spent eight years sailing the high seas with Disney Cruise Line first as a performer and then as an Entertainment Manager. Kim wrote this book for her dad and brother and for all the amazing fathers and father figures out there. It's a follow up to her first book "Honey I Love You" all about a mother's love. She hopes these books contribute to the love and connection between parents and kids for years to come!

Nabeel Hayder – Illustrator: Nabeel is an experienced illustrator who lives in Pakistan. He specializes in water colour illustrations for children's books. He loves helping to bring stories to life through his art.

If you love "Kiddo I Love You" you're sure to love "Honey I Love You"! It's available on Amazon and Indigo.ca.

Follow Kim on Social Media to keep up to date on upcoming books!
@kimbunka.author on Instagram and Tik Tok
Kim Bunka - Author on Facebook